ISBN 0 361 06277 X

Published 1984 by Purnell Books, Paulton,
Bristol BS18 5LQ, a member of the BPCC group.
Phototypeset by Quadraset Limited
Made and printed in Great Britain

Toy Box Tales

Stories by Jane Carruth

Illustrations by Diane Matthes

Purnell

Panda's Wonderful Idea

Some of the toys in Simon's toybox were worried.

"Are you sure Simon is properly asleep?" asked Panda.

"Of course he is asleep," said Elephant.

"Then let's have a meeting," said Teddy, who was the oldest.

Curly, the little white lamb, and Zoey, the black cat, sat down together. They were friends. Gerry, the giraffe, and Lennie Leopard joined them on the floor at the foot of Simon's bed.

Teddy began the meeting. "Some of us heard Simon's Mummy say that there were too many of us. She said that Simon must give one of us away."

"Oh dear, I-I'm s-sure it is g-going to be m-me," whispered little Curly. "Simon doesn't often play with me now."

Then Panda said, "I have an idea. We could hide in the wardrobe and under the bed. So none of us will be here when Simon comes looking for us."

Everybody thought Panda's idea was simply wonderful. And they set about finding hiding-places.

Can you see them?

The next morning when Simon went to his toybox he found it was empty.

"I wonder where they can be hiding?" Mummy said. "I expect this is their way of telling us they all want to stay together." Then she smiled. "Why don't we keep all the toys until Aunty Margaret's new baby is your age. Then we can give him your toys all at once!"

Mary Annabella Rose

Mary Annabella Rose was a very proud doll. She wore a splendid satin dress with frills and bows, and when she went out for walks with Susan, she wore a straw bonnet trimmed with flowers.

None of Susan's other dolls really liked her. Jemima said she was too proud. And Mirabella called her, "Miss Nose-in-the-air." Now it is true that Mary Annabella Rose was proud but she did so want to have friends. "What CAN I do to make the others like me?" she asked Owlet, who always sat on the window ledge quite close to the toybox.

"I'll tell you what to do," said Owlet, in his best hooting kind of voice. "You should ask Jemima and Mirabella to tea. And when they come, don't talk about yourself and don't start saying your dresses are prettier than anything they have."

"Yes, Owlet, thank you for your advice. I'll ask them today," said Mary Annabella Rose.

Jemima and Mirabella were very surprised when Mary Annabella Rose invited them to tea, and then praised their nice dresses. Then she said, "Please tell me all about yourselves."

Jemima told her story and then Mirabella told hers, and by the end of the afternoon they were all talking and laughing.

"I like Mary Annabella Rose after all," said Jemima. "I can't think why I didn't like her before."

"I like her too," said Mirabella. "After all, she can't help it if she has to wear all these satin dresses. And didn't we have a lovely conversation? I hope she invites us to tea again."

Now Mary Annabella Rose is very happy. She has two lovely friends and no one ever thinks of calling her "Miss Nose-in-the-air".

The Little Yellow Duck

This is a story about a little yellow duck. He was made of wool and he was very soft and cuddly. When William got him for a birthday present, the first thing he did was to ask his Mummy if he could give the little yellow duck a swim in the bath.

"I'm afraid not, darling," said Mummy. "Your duck is made of wool."

Now the little yellow duck was longing to have a swim.

That night he told some of his friends in the toybox about it. "You can't," said one of the bears. "You're made of wool."

The next night, when

William was having his bath, William's Mummy carried the little duck into the bathroom.

"There," she said. "You can sit on the bathroom stool and keep William company."

Well, somehow or other the little yellow duck managed to get himself on to the edge of the bath and then topple in!

Goodness — the water was full of soapy bubbles which got into his eyes! It was horrid.

Just then Mummy came in, and William cried, "Yellow duck has fallen into the water. Help me find him!"

The little yellow duck was so pleased to be on dry land again — sitting in front

of the fire on a big bath mat — that he made up his mind never to go swimming again.

So now he is very content to be taken for walks in William's little go-cart!

The Toy Box Lady

Once upon a time there was a very nice, kind old lady who loved children but she didn't know any. So she bought a toyshop, and filled it with toys.

Soon, all the children

round about were bringing their Mummies and Daddies to visit the old lady's toyshop. And soon she had lots of friends among the children.

One day, a little boy came to the toyshop with his Mummy. He had a brown skin and he was very polite. "Would you like a big ball or perhaps a football?" said the nice, kind toyshop lady.

The little boy shook his head, and his Mummy said, "He doesn't know any children. He would have to play by himself."

"That's funny," said the

old lady. "Once I didn't know any children either." Then she thought for a bit. "I have an idea," she said at last. "You leave your little boy with me whilst you go shopping. Soon, lots of children will come to the shop. I'll see that they talk to him."

The little boy stayed with the old lady and he played with all the toys she gave him until some children came into the shop with their Mummies and Daddies. "Here is a little friend of mine who is lonely," said the kind old lady to one Daddy she knew quite well.

"Oh, I'm sure Peter would love to play with him in the garden," said Peter's Daddy. "I'll wait until his Mummy comes back. Then we can all go home together."

How pleased and happy the nice, kind old toyshop lady was when she heard this, and the little boy with the brown skin reached up and gave her a great big hug and a kiss. For now he had a new friend, thanks to her.

The Naughty Bears

Did you know that Father Christmas always went round his toy factory long before Christmas filling his big sacks? All the toys knew this. And some naughty pink and blue bears hid behind the boxes of jig-saw puzzles so that Father Christmas would not see them when he made his round. So, when it was time for Father Christmas to set out on his long journey there were no pink and blue little bears in his sack.

Well, when Father Christmas had gone some miles over the snow and ice he suddenly thought he would make sure he had the special rocking horse he had promised to bring to a little boy called Billy. Of course when he looked inside his sack he found there were no pink and blue bears!

"That's funny," said Father Christmas, scratching his long white beard. "No pink and blue bears and they have been promised to a whole lot of girls and boys!" And he turned his reindeer and drove back to the toy factory to find the bears.

The naughty bears were dancing about the factory floor and turning somersaults. They were having super fun!

"Don't you know it's nearly Christmas!" shouted Father Christmas. "You are all meant for presents."

"We want to stay here," said one pink bear, dancing up and down.

"We don't want to be presents," said one blue bear. "Anyway, you will have to catch us."

But Father Christmas was not listening. He got a big net and threw it over all the naughty little bears. Then he took them outside in the net and emptied them into his big sack just as if they were all little fishes.

"We did have fun!" said the little bears, once they were inside the sack. "So now we had better be good and turn ourselves into nice presents. After all it is nearly Christmas!"

You can be sure that all the boys and girls who found pink and blue bears in their pillow-cases had no idea that the sweet little bears had once been very naughty bears!

Tootles comes to Tea

Poppy, the rag doll, and Jack Sailor were just sitting down to tea when the door of the playroom was pushed open. Koko Clown on the rocking horse was the first to notice the stranger come in.

"What is it?" Koko asked Poppy and Jack Sailor. "Look, it walks on four legs and it is all spotty."

Poppy gave a little scream and Jack Sailor said bravely, "I'll look after you. Don't be frightened."

The spotted 'thing' on four legs and with long floppy ears waddled over to Jack Sailor, who said quickly, "Go away, whatever you are! We don't want you here!"

Poppy began to give little screams again. Just then in came Trevor. "Tootles, you bad, bad dog!" he cried. "I lost you!" And he bent down and gathered the fat little puppy in his arms.

When Poppy saw that the 'thing' wasn't really coming to tea, she began

to smile. And Jack Sailor whispered, "It's only a puppy. If Trevor leaves him, perhaps we *could* ask him to tea."

Now human boys don't understand what toys say when they speak to each other, but dogs and cats always do. So Tootles knew that he was invited to tea if he liked to stay. "Woof, woof!" he said to Jack Sailor, as his master began stroking his soft coat. "I'll come to tea just as soon as I can get away." And when Trevor's Mummy called him and told him to shut Tootles in the playroom, Snuffles found he could go to tea with Poppy and Jack Sailor after all.

The Fiercest Growliest Tiger

The fiercest, growliest tiger that ever was lived in Jeremy's toybox. He had a gorgeous black and yellow striped coat and long whiskers and a terrible growl. ''I am a tiger,'' he would growl every now and then. ''All you other toys must do what I say.''

The big elephant got very tired of tiger always growling and telling him what to do. ''I'm bigger than you,'' he said. ''And I have a trunk which you haven't got. I can do things with my trunk which you can't do.''

This made the tiger very

cross and he growled more fiercely than ever. But the elephant only laughed.

One day, when Jeremy was out with his Mummy, the elephant went into the kitchen. He filled his trunk with water he found in a pail. Then he went back to the nursery. The tiger growled and growled at him and the elephant lifted his trunk and splashed the tiger all over with water.

What a fright the tiger had! He was so scared he forgot to growl.

"Let that be a lesson to you," said the elephant. "If you growl at me again, I'll splash you with water."

Well, the fiercest, growliest tiger soon learnt to change his growl into a soft, purring kind of growl and all the other toys were able to do what they wanted instead of what HE wanted.

Of course, Jeremy and his Mummy couldn't understand the water on the nursery floor. And the elephant and the tiger were not going to tell them how it got there!

The Little Blue Car

The little blue car sat in the very front of Mr. Dickson's window all over Christmas. It was still there — weeks and weeks after Christmas — and it was feeling very sad and lonely.

Every time David and his Mummy passed the toyshop, David looked at the little blue car and wished it was his.

"You will have to wait until it's your birthday," Mummy said.

"But it might be sold by then," said David. "My birthday is not for ages and ages."

When it was nearly Easter, David's Granny came to stay. David often helped to carry her parcels and find her ball of wool when she lost it under the chair.

On the day she was going back home, David's Granny said, "Now, David, I would like to give you a little present . . ."

And David said, "I have lots of toys in my toybox but I haven't got a little blue car."

David took his Granny to the toyshop and he was so pleased when he saw that the little blue car was still in the front of the window. It looked very dusty, but he didn't mind. And Mr. Dickson, the toyshop man, didn't mind selling it. "I'll let you have it half price," he said. "It's been in the window so long."

Now the little blue car is no longer sad or lonely. David plays with him every single day.

Teddy Edward Bear and his Family

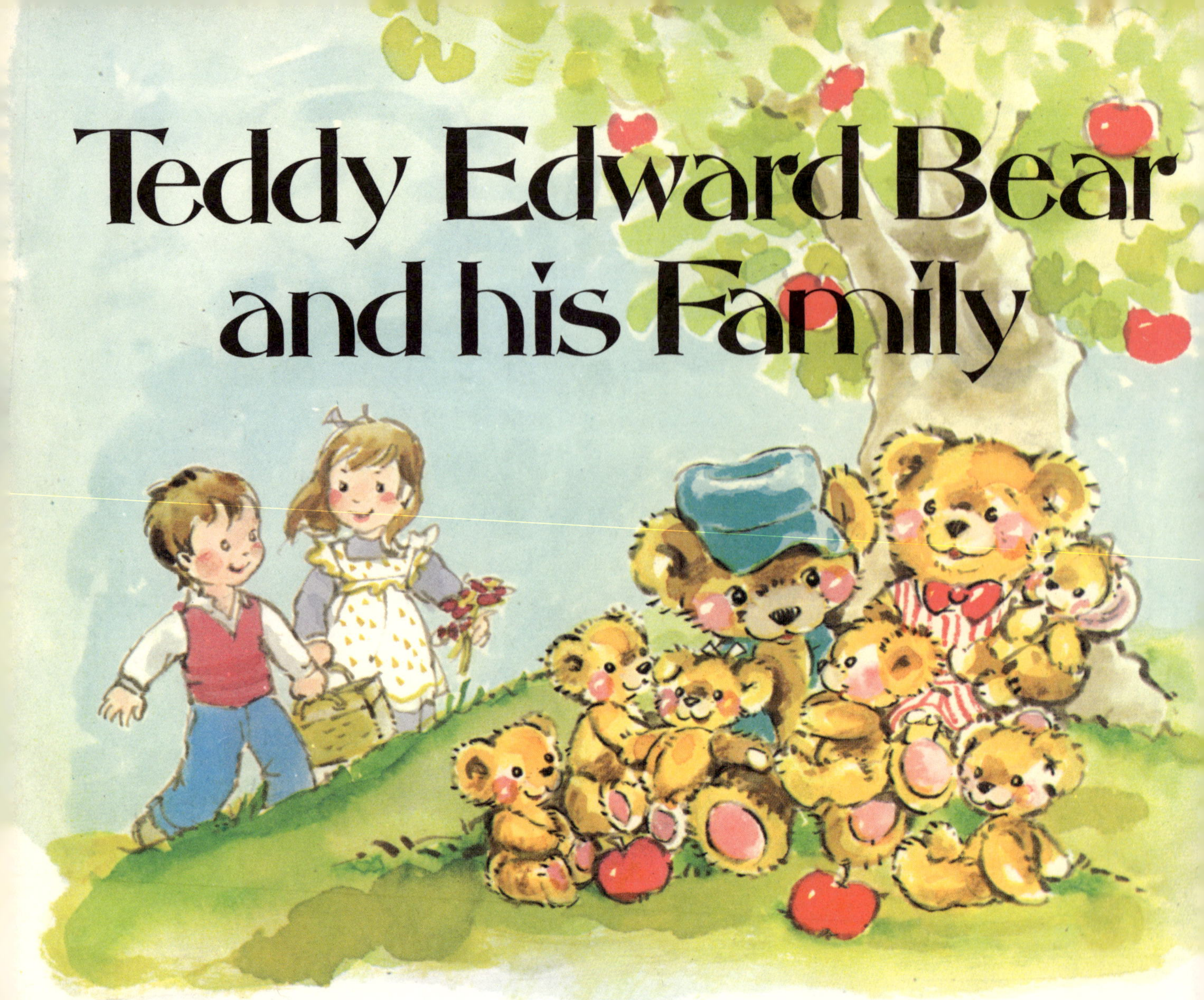

Teddy Edward Bear was head of the family. He was very proud of his wife and children and liked to take them out for an airing when the sun was shining. One afternoon, he was sitting under the apple tree with all his six children round him. He wore a smart blue cap and his best red and white spotted bow tie.

"Now then, children," he said. "Sit up straight. Look your best. We are all going to have a picnic tea with Charles and Sarah."

Soon, Charles and Sarah came along with the picnic basket which held all the food. Then Sarah spread a pretty flowered cloth on the grass and set out the food.

"There are honey sandwiches for you bears," she said.

"And chocolate cake for us," said Charles.

Teddy Edward Bear was very proud of his children because they behaved so well and, at the end of the picnic, Sarah fetched her big pram and gave all the Bear children a ride round the garden whilst Teddy Edward Bear and Charles had a grown-up conversation about the weather underneath the old apple tree.

The Toys have a Holiday

Once upon a time there was a little girl called Laura. One day she asked her Mummy if she could give her toys a holiday. "I don't see why not," said Mummy. "It's a lovely sunny day." Mummy got out Laura's old pram. And Laura went off to tell Judy and Wendy and all the cuddly toys that they were going on holiday. "We're going to the seaside for the day," she told them.

What a wonderful day it was. Judy and Wendy sat on top of Laura's sandcastle, and Bunny Rabbit and Puss-Cat and Panda sat on the rug whilst Laura read to them from her book of Fairy Tales.

At the end of the holiday, Laura and her Mummy

pushed them home in the pram and put them all to bed.

Just before Judy closed her eyes, she whispered to Wendy. ''I wish we had a holiday every day, don't you?''

''Of course I do,'' said Wendy. ''Now be quiet and go to sleep!''

Mok the Monkey

Mok, the little monkey with the red cap and the red waistcoat, was not a very happy little monkey. He had played so many tricks on his friends that they didn't even want to share their toybox with him.

"I'll be good," said Mok. "I promise!"

"That is what you said the last time — after you had tipped the ink bottle over me," said Bruff, the little brown dog.

"Then you tied some string on my beautiful tail," said Flossie, the ginger cat.

"I really will be good," said Mok. "Let's all be friends again."

But none of the toys really believed him until one day Mok found an old music box.

"What is it?" asked Bruff.

None of the toys knew

except clever Mok. He told them to get ready for a jolly dance. Then he climbed up on top of the table with the music box and began turning the handle. The music box played so many lovely tunes that soon all the toys were hopping and skipping in time to the music. Mok turned the handle until his arm began to hurt but he didn't stop.

"Thank you, Mok," said Bruff.

"Now we know you can do other things as well as play tricks," said Flossie. "So let's be friends again."

Mok was very happy when he heard this. "I'll make music for you again," he said.

Then Flossie and Bruff invited him to come home with them, and you can just imagine how pleased the little monkey was to be back in the toybox.

The Grand Ball

There was once a pretty young doll who had nothing to wear when the King of Toyland sent her an invitation to his Grand Ball.

"What shall I do?" she asked her friends in the toy-box.

The doll's name was Pippa and her two friends were called Jasmine and Geraldine. "I tell you what," said Jasmine, after she had thought for a long time, "you must find something we can make into a dress."

"That's a good idea," said Geraldine. "We'll have a look round the nursery tonight when everybody is asleep."

It was lucky that there was a bright moon shining in the sky that night. The nursery was full of moonlight as Pippa and Jasmine and Geraldine began their search. Pippa found some white socks but they were no use. Geraldine found some hair ribbon but that was no use. And then, at last, Jasmine found a lovely big square of white cotton covered all over with pretty coloured flowers.

Pippa stood up straight whilst her two friends held up the pretty square in front of her. And then they began to cut, snip, snip and stitch. Soon the cotton square was a lovely dress.

Pippa tried it on and she was thrilled. "Now I can go to the King's Grand Ball," she cried.

Pippa and Jasmine and Geraldine had a wonderful time at the Grand Ball and the King said Pippa's dress was quite charming.

I wonder if Pippa's little mistress is still looking for that cotton square with the flowers on it?